NOW YOU CAN READ ABOUT....
PLANES

Written by Marjorie Rogers

Illustrated by Tony Gibbons

BRIMAX BOOKS · NEWMARKET · ENGLAND

For many years men have wanted to fly like the birds. Some tried by fitting wings to their arms and jumping off high places. Some filled balloons with hot air and floated in them. They could not stay up in the air.

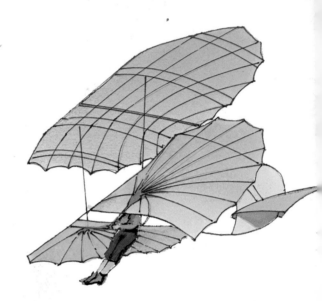

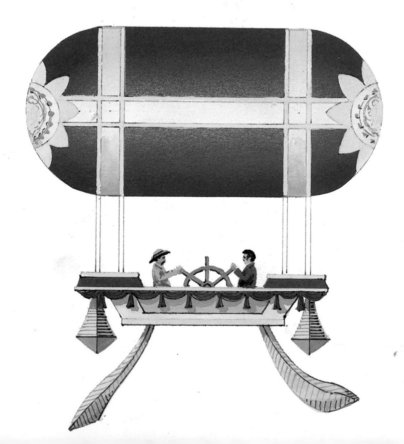

Men found that a plane must have
wings to lift it, a tail to keep
it steady and an engine to give
it power. Over seventy years ago
in America, an engine was fitted
into a glider. The first short
flight was made.
Planes can now fly all over the
world and even out into space.

This is an airport. Planes need
runways for taking-off and
landing. Can you see the planes?
Some are in parking bays or gates.
This is where people get on or off
the planes. Before taking-off, a
plane will need fuel.

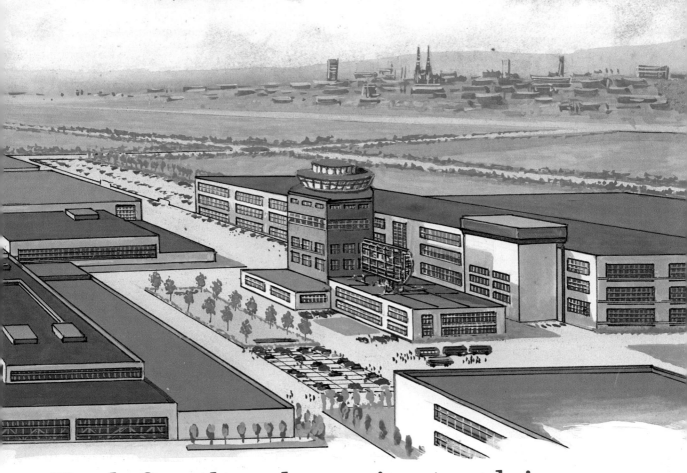

Fuel for the planes is stored in
big tanks on the airport.
Airports are very busy places.
Many people work there. They take
care of the people who fly in and
out every day and night. On the
airport there are large buildings.
There people can wait for flights,
shop and have meals.

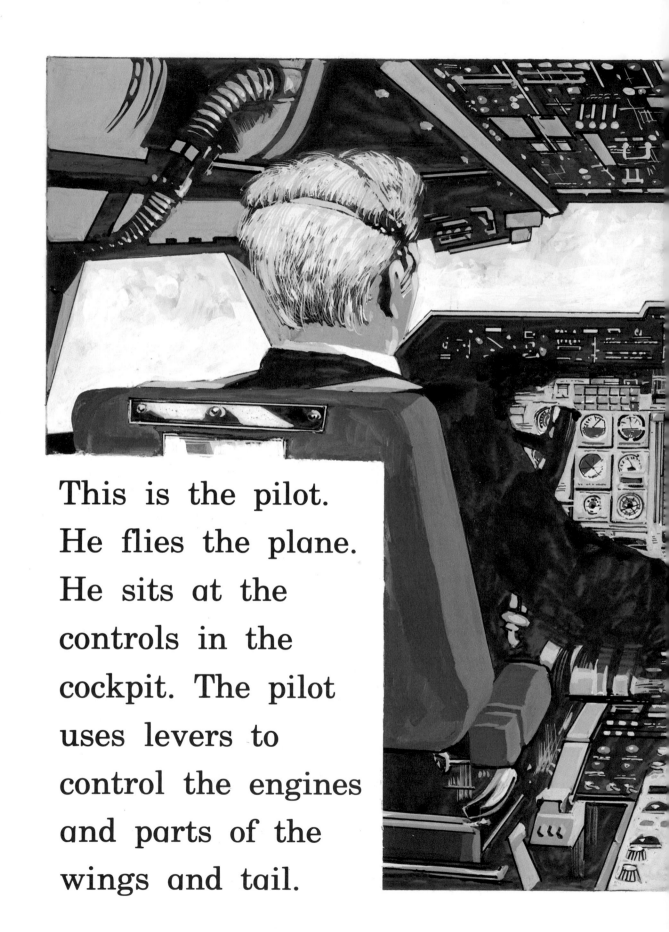

This is the pilot.
He flies the plane.
He sits at the
controls in the
cockpit. The pilot
uses levers to
control the engines
and parts of the
wings and tail.

Look at all the dials. They show
the pilot what the plane is
doing as it flies. The man
who sits with the pilot to help
him is called the co-pilot.

This is the control tower. The people who work here help the pilot. They can speak to the pilot of each plane over the radio.

They make sure that all the planes take-off and land on the right runway. They tell the pilot all about the weather. There is a plane ready for take-off.

The people who travel in an airliner sit in the cabin. The cabin crew serve food and drinks during the flight.

On long flights, you can watch a film and listen to music.
Under the floor of the cabin is the hold. This is where all the bags and cargo are stored.

Concorde is a very special plane. It has swept back wings and a droop nose. It can fly very fast and very high.

This plane has a very wide body. It is called a Jumbo Jet. It has seats for hundreds of people. This kind of plane is known as an airliner.

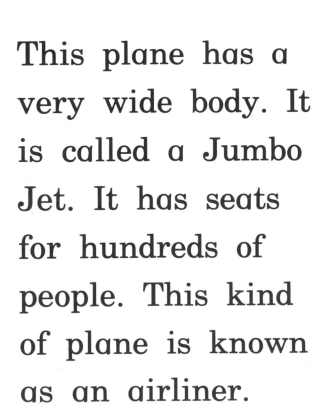

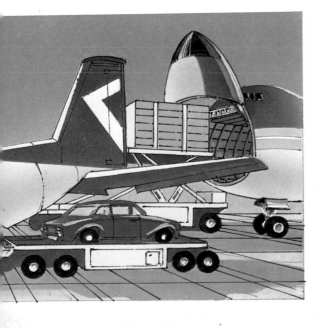

The Jump jet does not need a runway. It takes-off and lands straight down on the ground. It is the first jet that can do this.

A cargo plane can open at the front or back. It can carry heavy loads.

This plane has a metal body built like a fast boat. It can land and take-off on the sea, to ferry goods and people over the water. It is a sea-plane.

A helicopter is lifted into the sky by its blades. It can hover using the blades and the engine to keep it steady. It can be used to save people in danger.

Only one person can fly in this plane. It is used to spray crops. Spraying kills pests and weeds.

This airliner is inside a large building. It is called a hangar. Here many men work to make the plane ready to fly. All the parts of the plane must be in working order.

After a flight, repairs to the plane
can be made in the hangar. This
is to make sure that the plane
is safe to fly once more.

The first rockets to the moon
were only used once. The space
shuttle has been made so that
men can use it again and again.
It will be able to shuttle
between the earth and a space
station.

In the next few years, who knows at what speed planes will fly or what they will look like. Perhaps they will look like these.

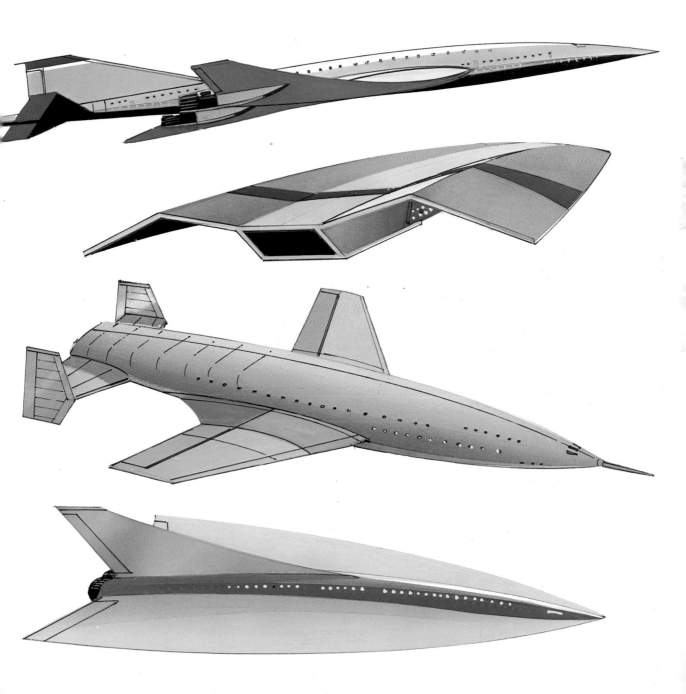

Can you name these? What kind of planes are they?

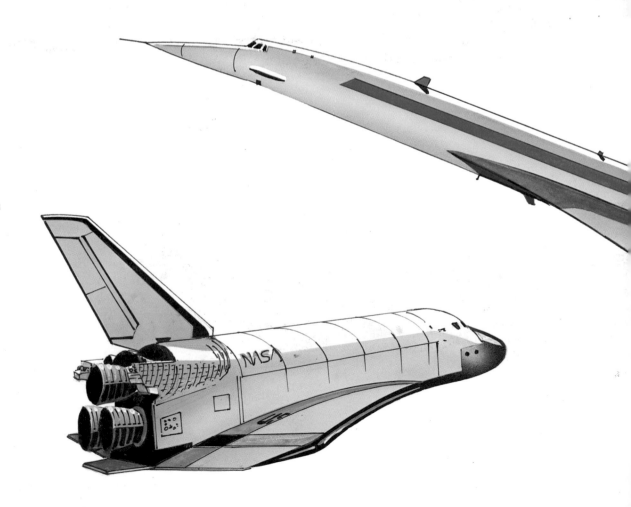